Learn How to Draw C
For the Beginn

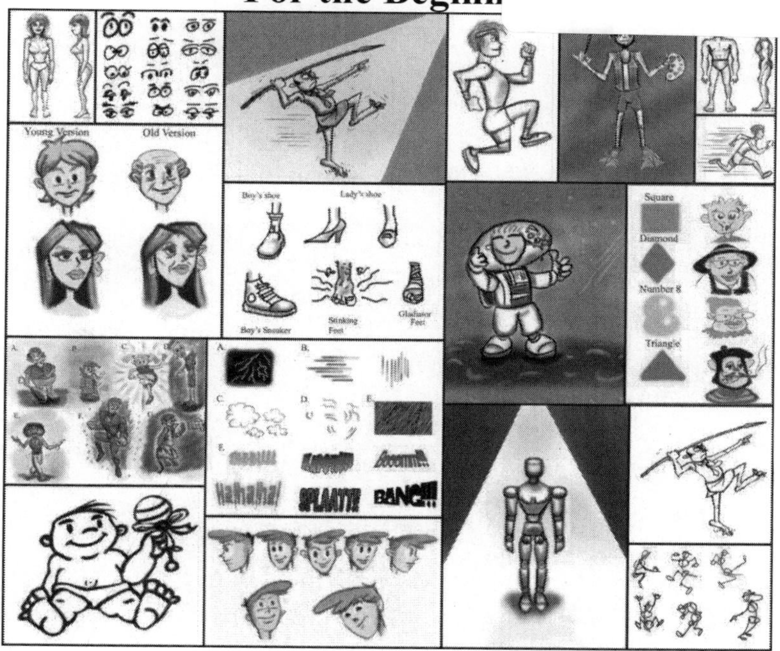

Step by Step Guide to Drawing Cartoons

Paolo Lopez de Leon
And
John Davidson

Learn to Draw Book Series

JD- Biz Publishing

All Rights Reserved.
No part of this publication may be reproduced in any form or by any means, including scanning, photocopying, or otherwise without prior written permission from JD-Biz Corp and at http://JD-Biz.com.
Copyright © 2014
All Images Licensed
By: Paolo Lopez de Leon
Learn How to Draw Books for the Beginner
http://learntodrawbooks.com

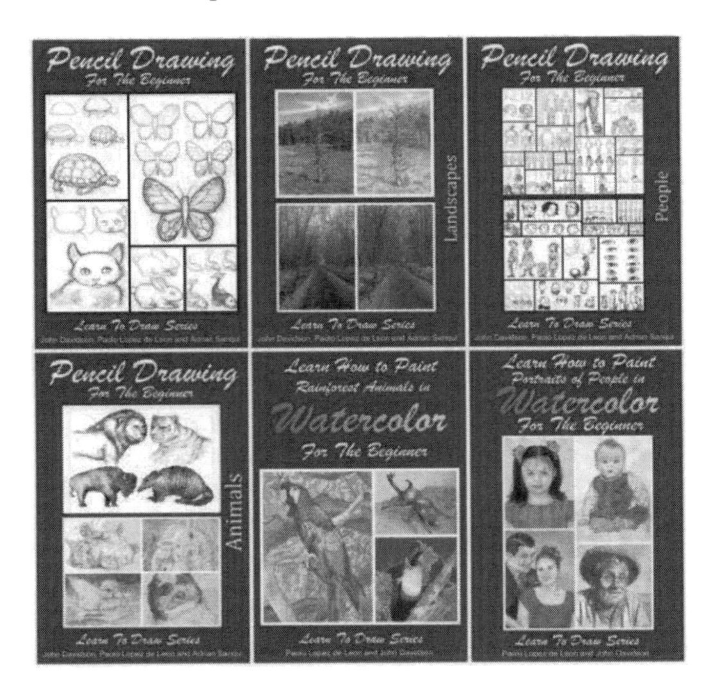

TABLE OF CONTENTS

Introduction:

Cartoons reminds me of Saturday morning when I was little, I usually bring along paper and pencil in front of our television, when the cartoon program starts, I drew along the characters in the paper, If I remember it right the show was about a munching sphere head who likes to eat pellets, when he eats the big pellet, that's the time he can eliminate his ghost enemies, I'm pretty sure you know that one, a popular video game anyway, after I drew it, when First day of School comes, I show it to my friends telling them how I spend my weekend, of course other than studying my lessons. So that was my Saturday morning cartoon days, now a days we have different cartoons, with a lot of selection or genre that some of it needs to have mature audience, that even a kid wouldn't relate to it, well that a contemporary trend, with a twisted style but at the end it can really entertain us, make us laugh and leave smiles to our faces.

Thanks for choosing this eBook as your guide in the world of cartoons, where you will experience how to draw your own cartoons, practicing the steps in the drawing procedures will help you gain the drawing skills, that you will need to became a cartoonist, you will learn the proper materials that you will use when drawing cartoons, you will be able to draw cartoons with confidence, and seeing the simplicity behind every cartoon characters that you desire to draw, so set some time to commit yourself drawing cartoons with the help of this eBook, so have fun when drawing cartoons.

Materials:

Pencils

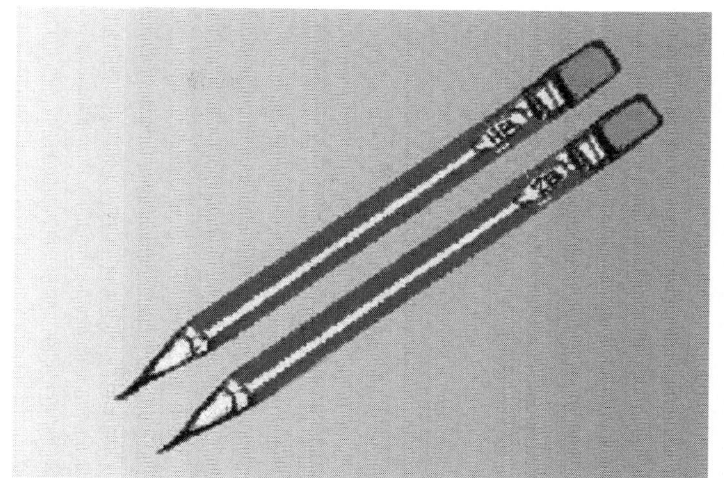

The most important tool, made from Graphite with a mixture of Clay, soft pencils like B have little amount of clay or not at all, used for outlining and giving texture to your drawing, comes in different scales: H(Hard), F, HB, and B(Soft) varying grades like 9H(lightest)to 9B(darkest)range.
For our drawings we need the following: HB and 2B, but if you're short of supplies, you can use HB only, just apply pressure when you want a darker tone and light pressure for light tone.

Mechanical Pencils

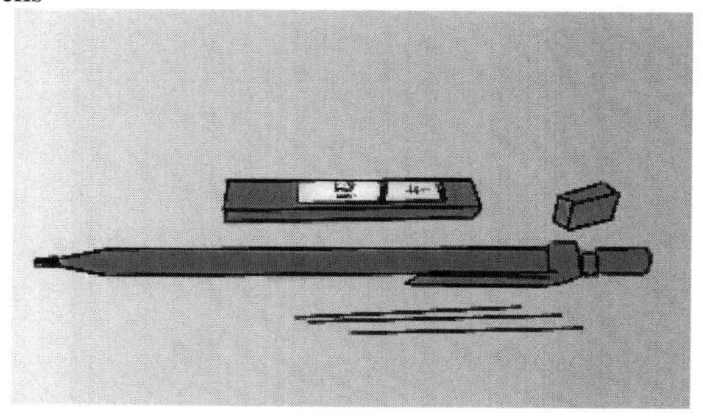

Like Pencils the lead is also made of Graphite, Good for details, come in handy especially for tight areas, the difference is it doesn't need a sharpener if the lead breaks, just press the cap on the end of the pencil and it's good to go, it comes in different sizes: 0.2mm to 5.6mm, for our drawing 0.5 will just be suffice.

Markers or Colored Pens

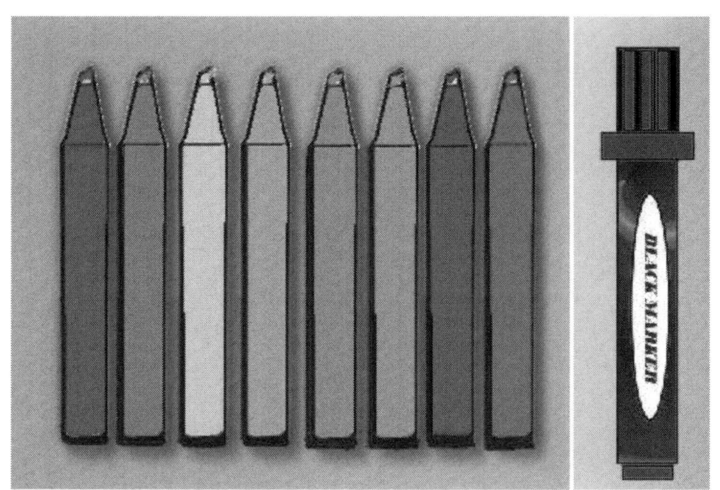

Used by Artist, Illustrator and Designer for coloring there works, sketch and illustrations, they are alcohol-based. Comes In different colors and the tip also come with a fine point, chisel and round shape. It depends which point is comfortable for you to use. For me I use the chisel point because it serve as a double purpose, if I want to render a thin line I would use the tip, and if I need a Broad stroke I'll use the side of the marker.

Sketchbook/ Bond paper/ Newsprint

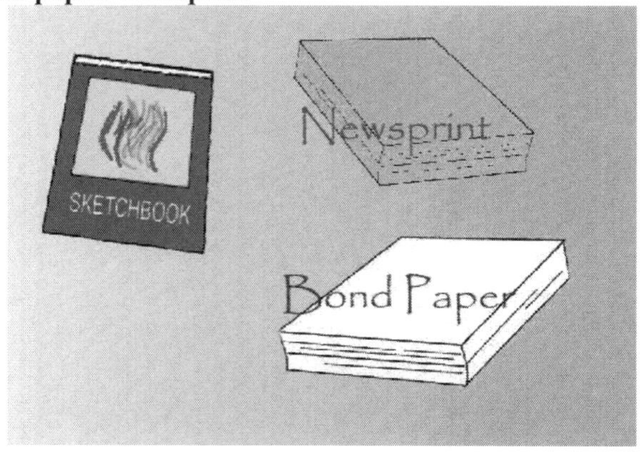

Since we're going to draw, we need a lot of paper for practice, and later on if we are very proficient, we're going to use more professional type of paper, but as of now let's stick to the less expensive kind of paper for a while which are Newsprint and Bond paper or white paper, sketchbook is good if you already learn the basic and you can do some loosely sketch with ease and you're more experience drawing cartoons, you can carry this around whenever you go, good when doing outdoor drawings, you can even show it to some of your friends or to other artist you know, so make sure it's portable to carry around(there are small sketchbook like a size of notebook that are available in any art store).

Erasers

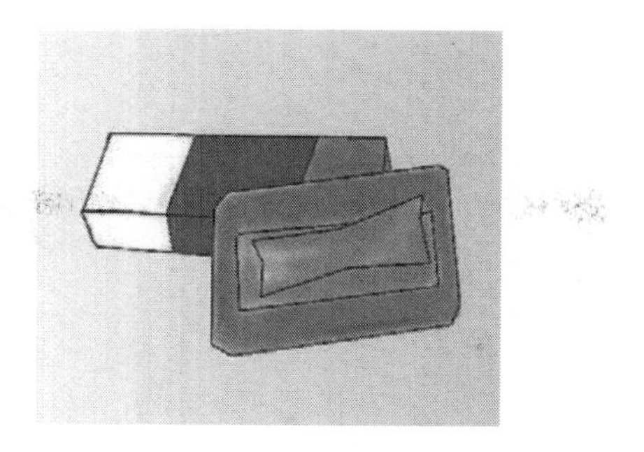

- **Kneaded Eraser**

This is like a clay or putty eraser, which can be mold to any difference shape and thickness, depending to your needs, it can lift Graphite in the paper without any damage, good for tight areas, can lighten areas in your drawing, and used for making highlights in your drawings to make it more realistic. Need to be replaced if it is already dark due to accumulation of Graphite.

- **Vinyl Eraser**

This kind of eraser does not smudge the surface of the paper; it can erase hard and tough areas totally especially for large areas, and does not harden.
There are other types of Erasers like Pink Eraser, Typewriter Erasers and Peel-Off type Eraser, you can also use those, as it depends on the availability of the materials in your area, feel free to experiment what works best for you.

Sharpener

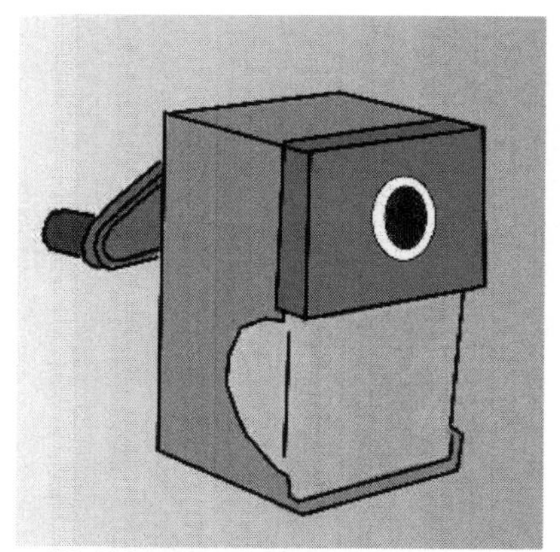

There is manual Sharpener, Wall-Mounted Sharpener and Electric Pencil Sharpener, Any type of Pencil sharpener will do, just make sure that it is safe to use. Use to sharpen the Pencil.

Ruler and Template

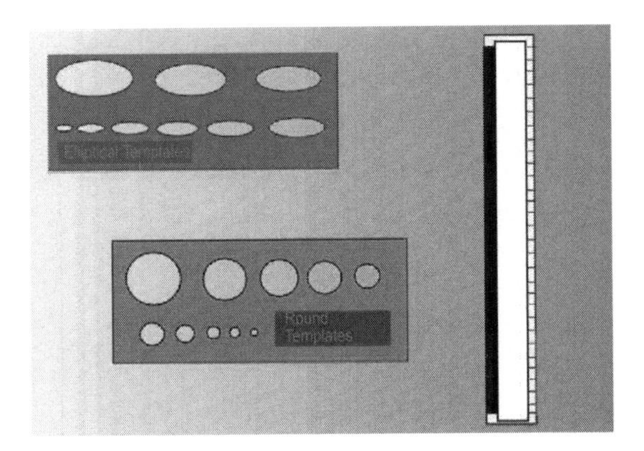

Ruler helps you draw straight lines, measure distance, you can use plastic or wooden for our drawings.
Templates can be use to draw circles or ellipse accurately, especially when drawing the parts of the eyes. Which demand a good form of shape.

Masking Tape or Artist Tape

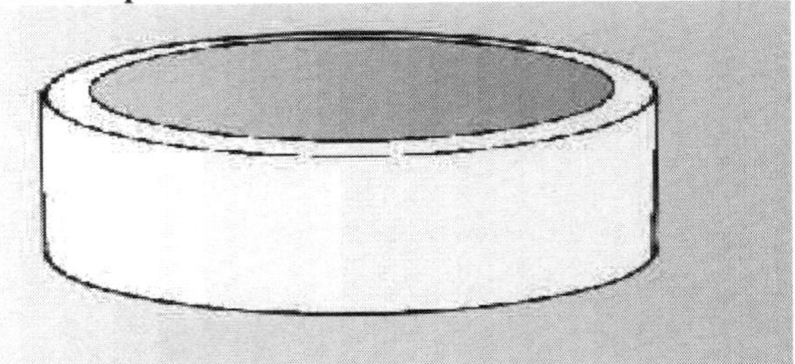

Use when you're going to attach your watercolor paper in the Masonite or Flexi-glass board.

Tracing Table or Light Table / Flexi-glass with Bendable Lamp

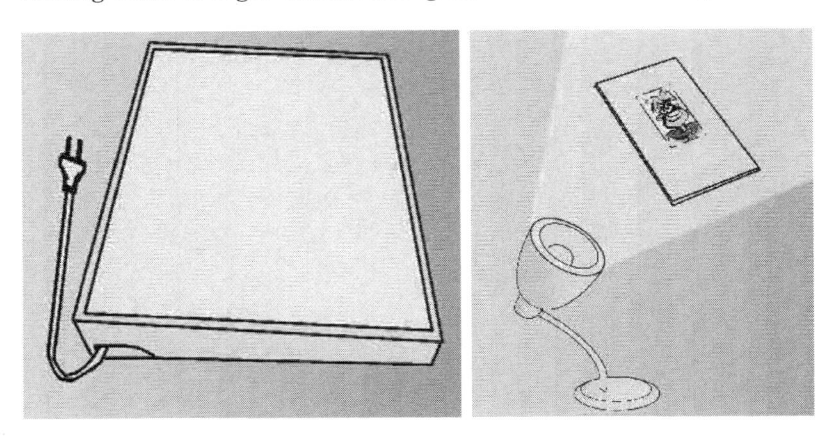

Tracing Table or Light Table use when tracing your draft or drawings to your other working paper to have a cleaner looks, place your drawings on the tracing table, with your working paper over it ("on the top of it") and trace the image. If ever you don't have a Tracing Table, you can improvise by using a clear Flexi-glass, ¼" thick and size that can accommodate your work, On a Horizontal Position (you can use chairs or anything that will support the Flexi-glass in that position), Place a bendable Lamp under it, turn it on (the idea is to place the light source at the back of the Flexi-glass so you can use it like a tracing table), mount your drawing or print and your working paper over the Flexi-glass(secure it with masking tape), and you have a tracing equipment, very simple that can save you Space, Time and Money. I see others made this kind of tracing table using ordinary box instead of finding chairs for support, so be creative.

Drawing a Cartoon Face:

Take your pencil (make sure it's sharp) and paper, and we're going to start to draw faces.

Man's Face

Steps:

1. Draw a big oval or oblong (use templates if you find it hard to draw the shape), notice that I made it more like an egg shape.

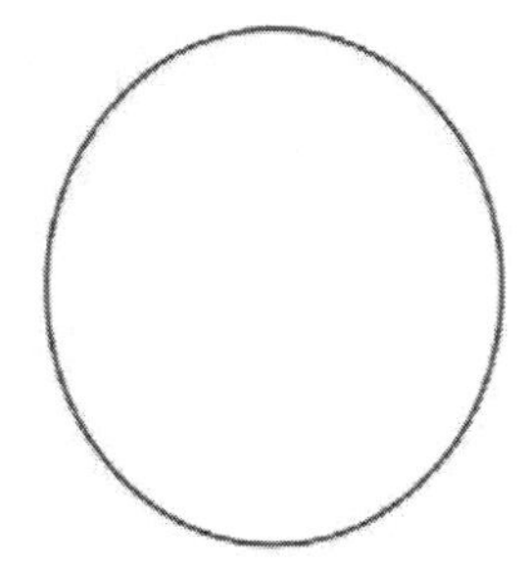

2. Next draw a two centerline like a crosshair, one is vertical and the other is horizontal.

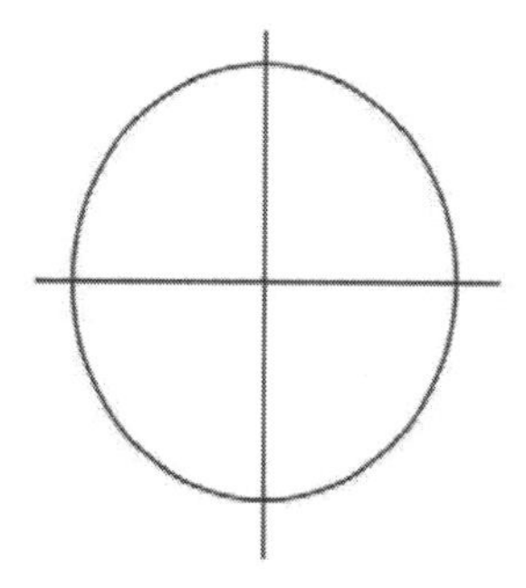

3. Draw a two small circles; one on the left side of the horizontal line and another to the right. This will be the eye.

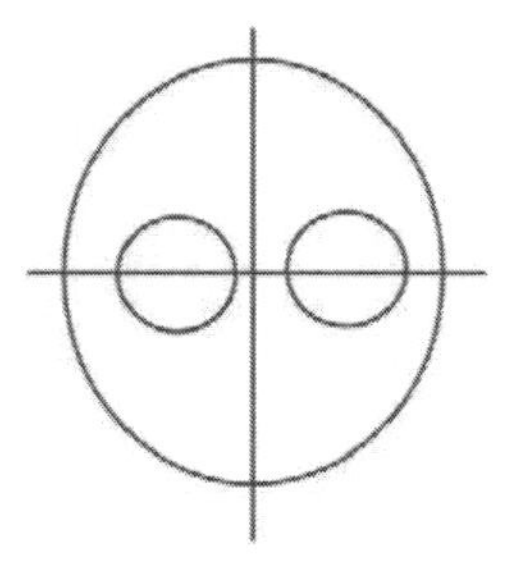

4. Below the eyes, on the lower vertical line, divide it to three parts, this will serve as a guide when drawing the nose, and the other line is for the mouth.

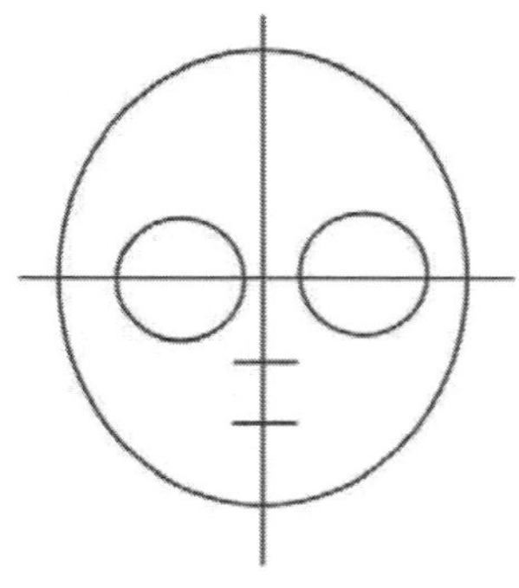

As you can see, we already have a guide for the face; we are still going to add more of it, so bear with me. And you just drew an alien face.

5. Let's draw the other parts: neck (a.), ear (b.), and a guide for the hair (c.) and (d.).

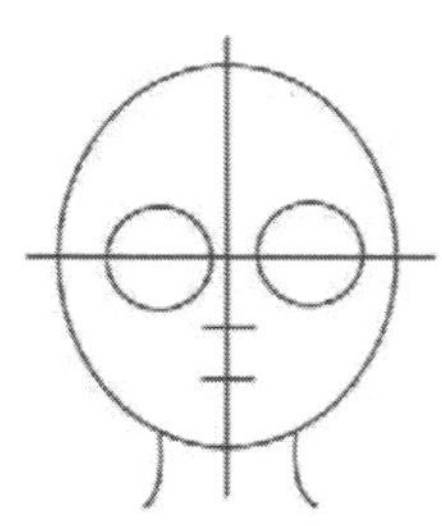

a.

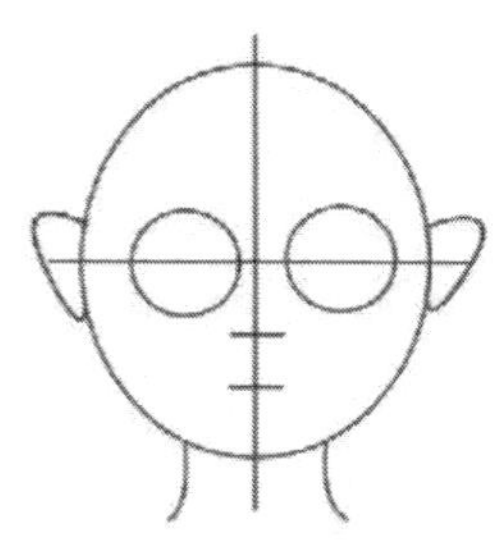

b.

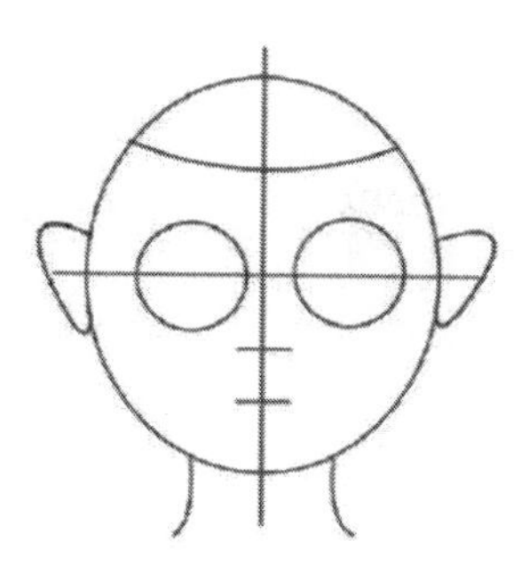

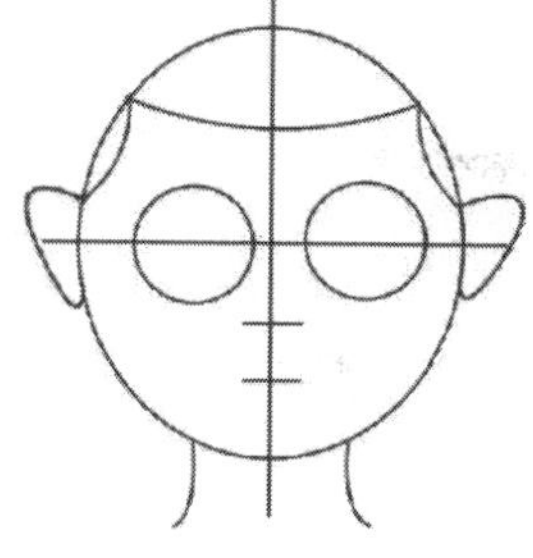

c. d.

6. Now let's draw necessary parts to make it more animate, start by adding the Iris (a.) and Pupil in the eyes (b.).

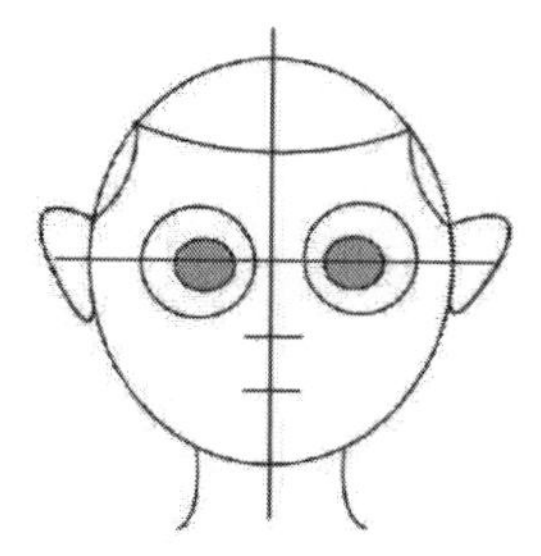

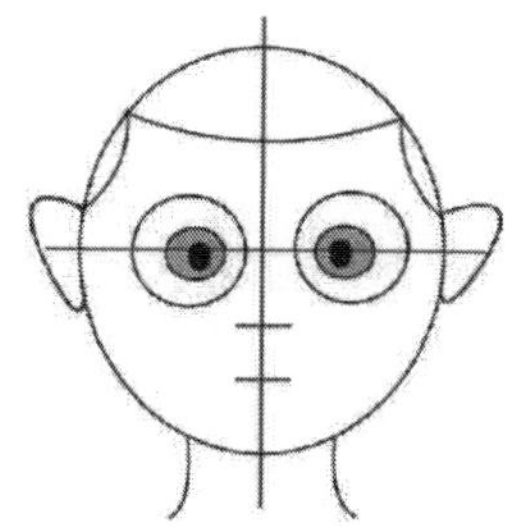

a. b.

I just add the color for the Iris as a mark, so that you will not get confuse, but don't worry later I'll fill the face with color.

7. Add the eyebrows for eyes (a.), nose (b.) and a smile (c.); you can now erase the guide.

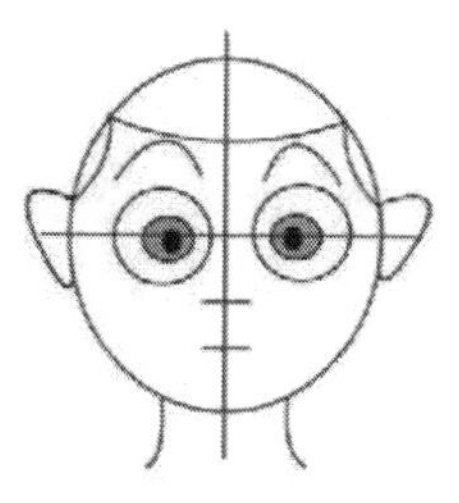

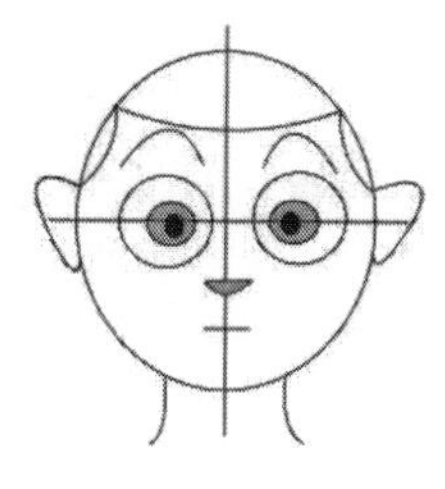

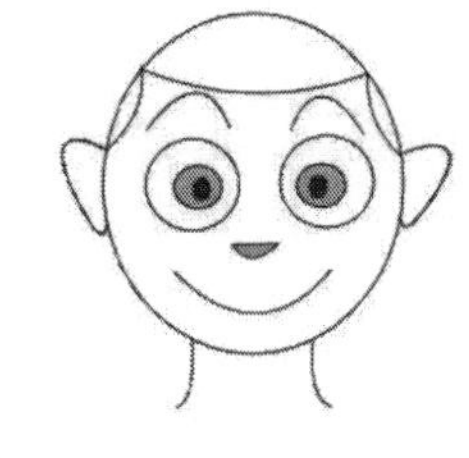

a. b. c.

8. We are not finish yet, let's make some improvement in his hairstyle to make him cool. I draw a guide on top of his head (a.) and erase the previous guide in the head (b.), this serves as an outline to where we will draw his hair. Next add the hair (c.) and add color the rest of the cartoon, Flesh color for the face and neck, gray for the hair, so this is how our cartoon face will look like with hair, and picture e., f., and g. show how the cartoon look like with various hairstyle.

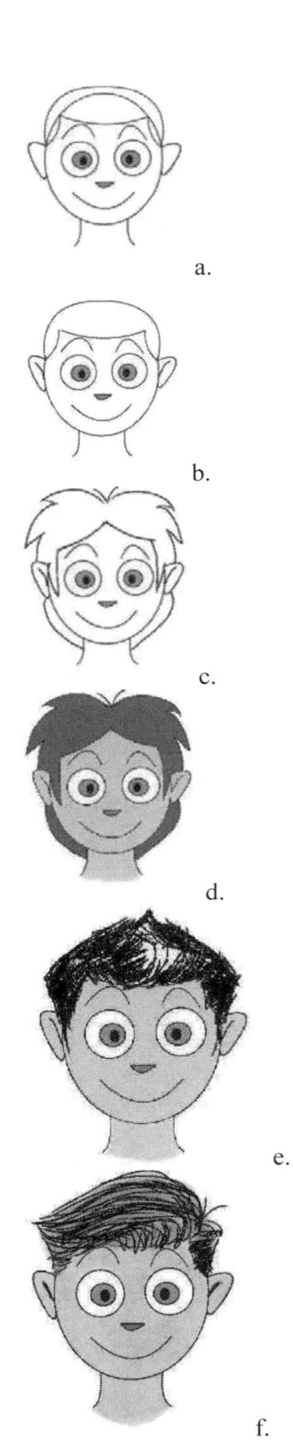
a.
b.
c.
d.
e.
f.

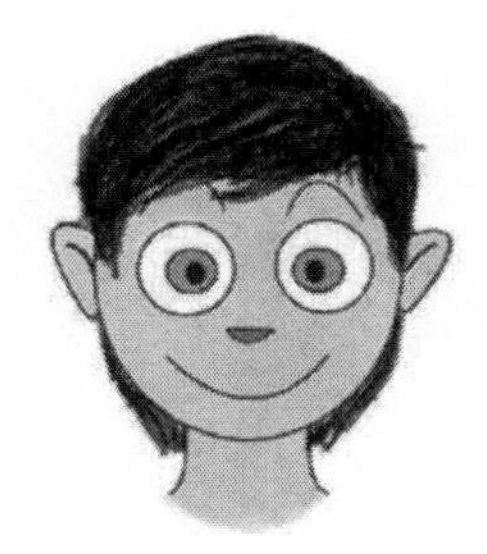

g.

Woman's Face

Steps:

1. Follow the steps 1-7 from Man's Face , and starting from the face features with hair guide (a.). Don't forget to color the iris using colored pen or marker.

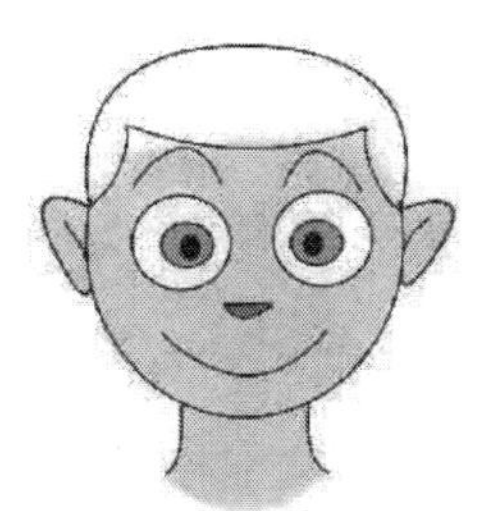

2. Draw eyelids for both eyes and also eyelashes.

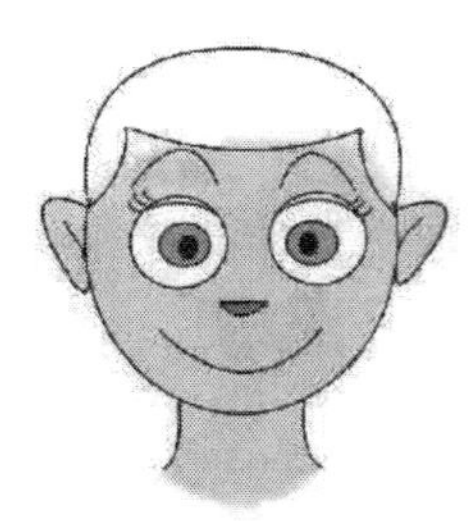

3. Add a full lip on that mouth area.

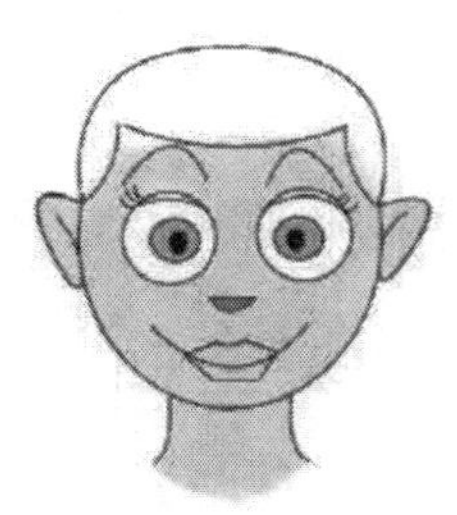

4. Add color to the lips (red) using colored pen, draw earrings and color it with yellow, and draw a ponytail.

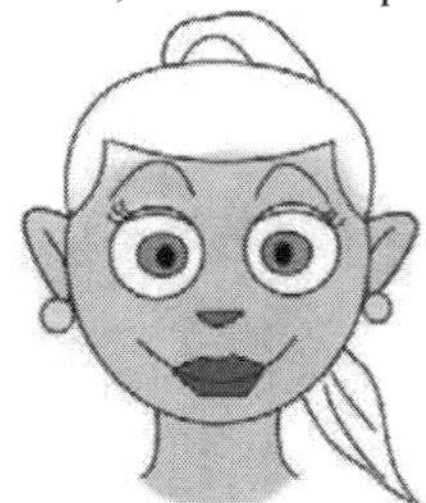

5. Color the hair with yellow first, then shade it with thin orange, and also paint the band behind the head with pink.

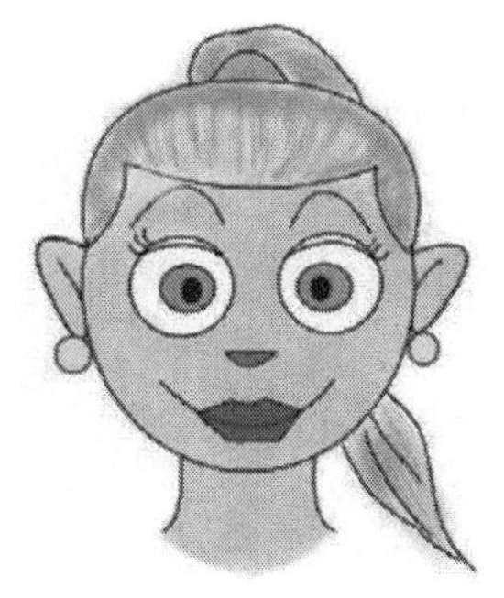

You can make a various kinds of hairstyles.

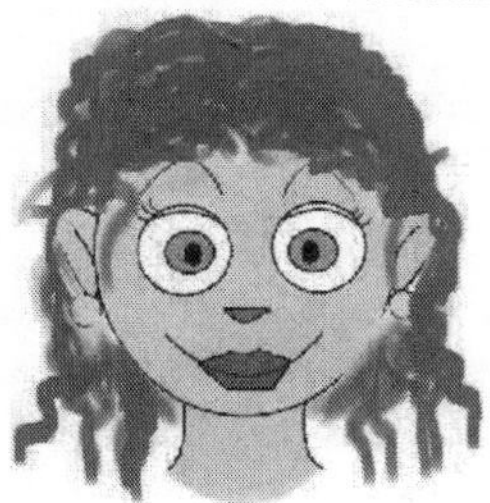

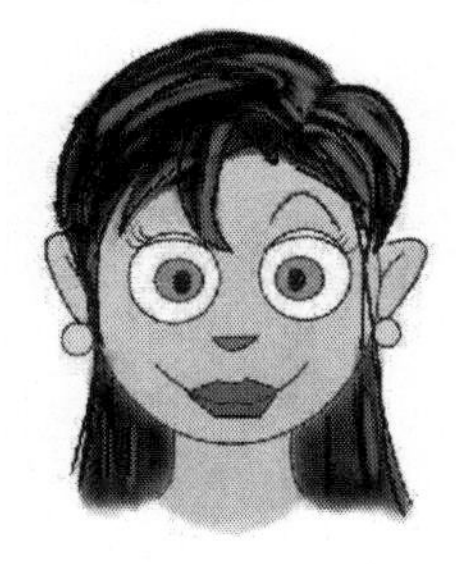

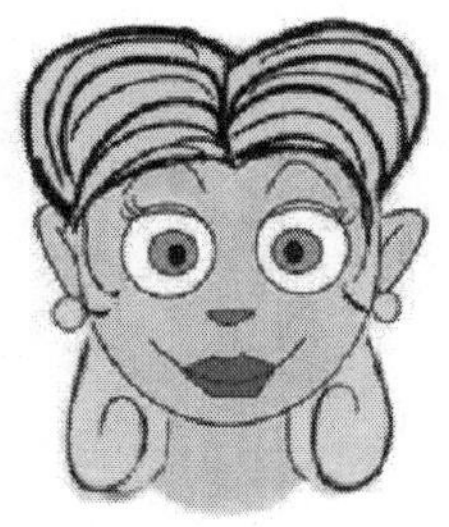

These cartoons Faces in our example above show you the basic and simple way to draw using basic shapes mostly circles and oblongs, as we move along I will show you how to make cartoons with other different style and shapes.

More about a Cartoons Face

Take note of the relationship when drawing the front view of your cartoon, when you're drawing its side view, notice the placement of the parts in the front view of the face are the same level with the parts in side view.

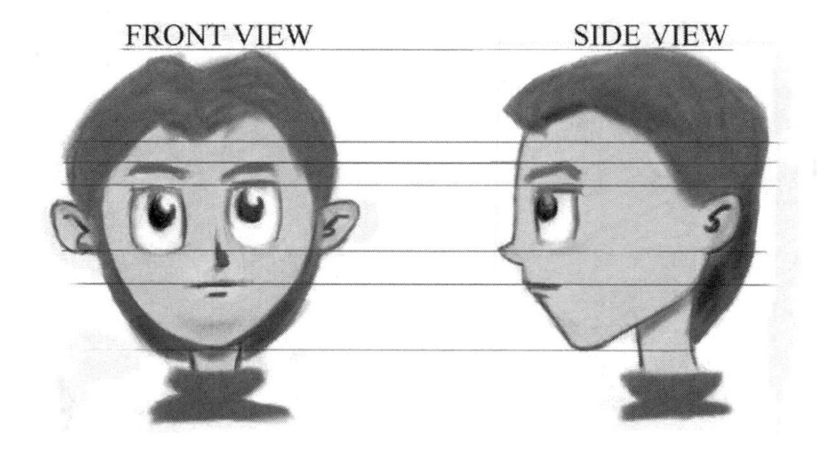

Different angles of the Face

The cartoons below shows you, how to draw the different sides of our redhead cartoon character including: Front view, three-quarter views left and right, side views left and right also, looking up and looking down. The character was drawn the same principles we drew the face in the topic drawing the cartoon face, the difference was that the redhead was drawn using freehand while the later one was drawn using templates or perfect circle.

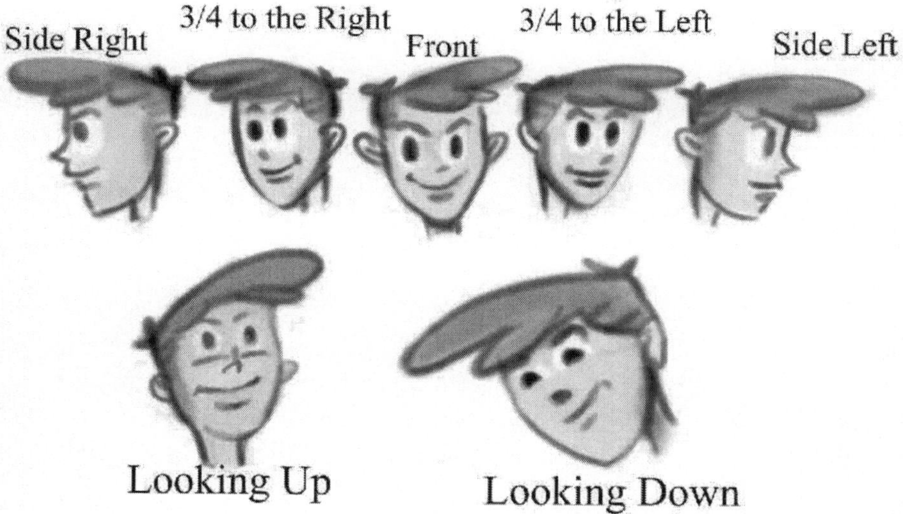

Steps:

1. Same as what we did in drawing the face of the man, start drawing the egg shape for the face, as you can see I intentionally draw it like an egg shape to have a good form later by just freehand.

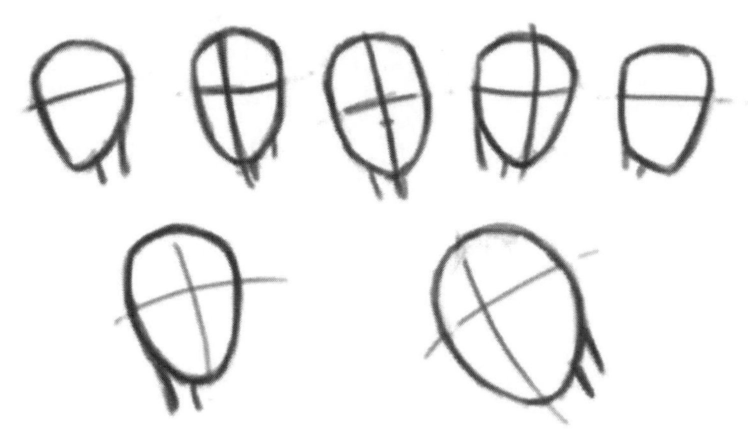

2. Next add the eyes, noses and mouths to all the views.

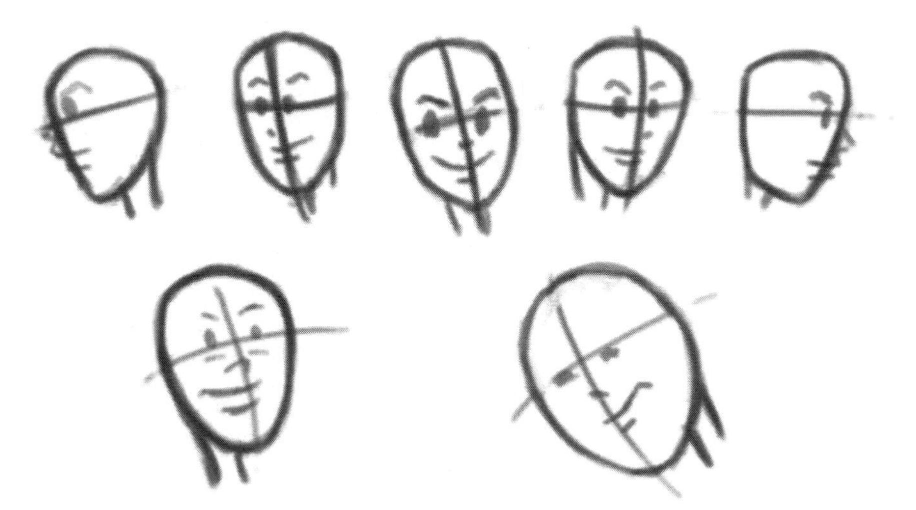

3. Finish the rest of the details in the hairs.

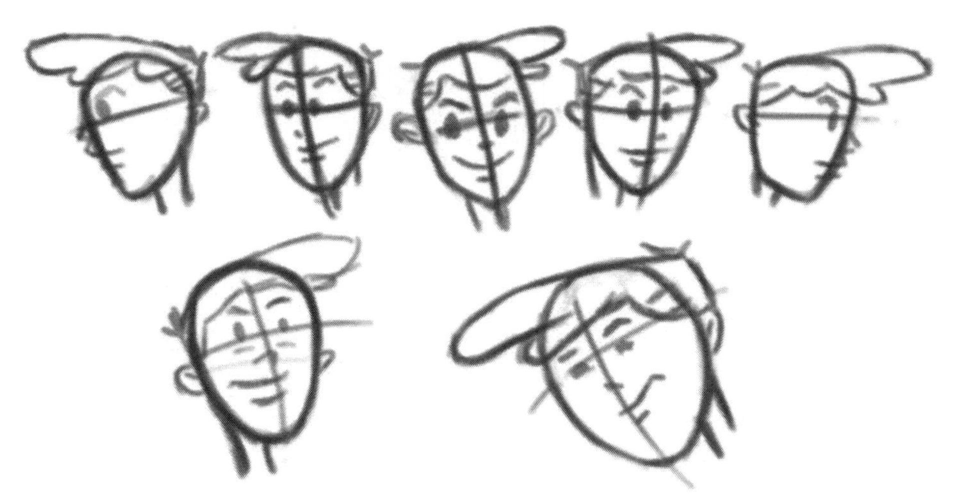

4. Erase the crosshairs, and add colors to all the views: flesh for the skins, red for the hairs, and leave the white of the eyes no need to color it.

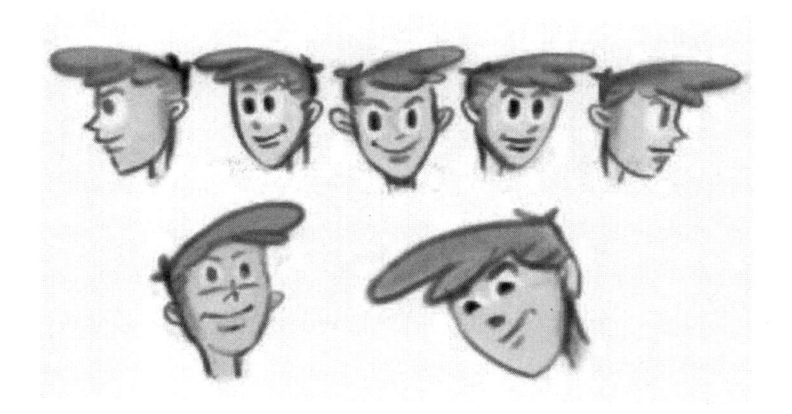

Practice drawing the picture above again using circles as your framework for the face; draw them in different sides for you to familiarize yourself drawing cartoons.

Different faces have Different shapes

We learn how to draw faces using circles as our main ingredient in drawing cartoon faces, well there are other cartoon faces that we can create using other shapes as you see below, the boy face has a square shape, the old pilgrim has a diamond face, the lady with a wide lips face has a shape like a number 8 and the French guy has a triangular shape face. The bottom line when drawing cartoons is to make it silly or wacky, as cartoons it supposed to be fun.

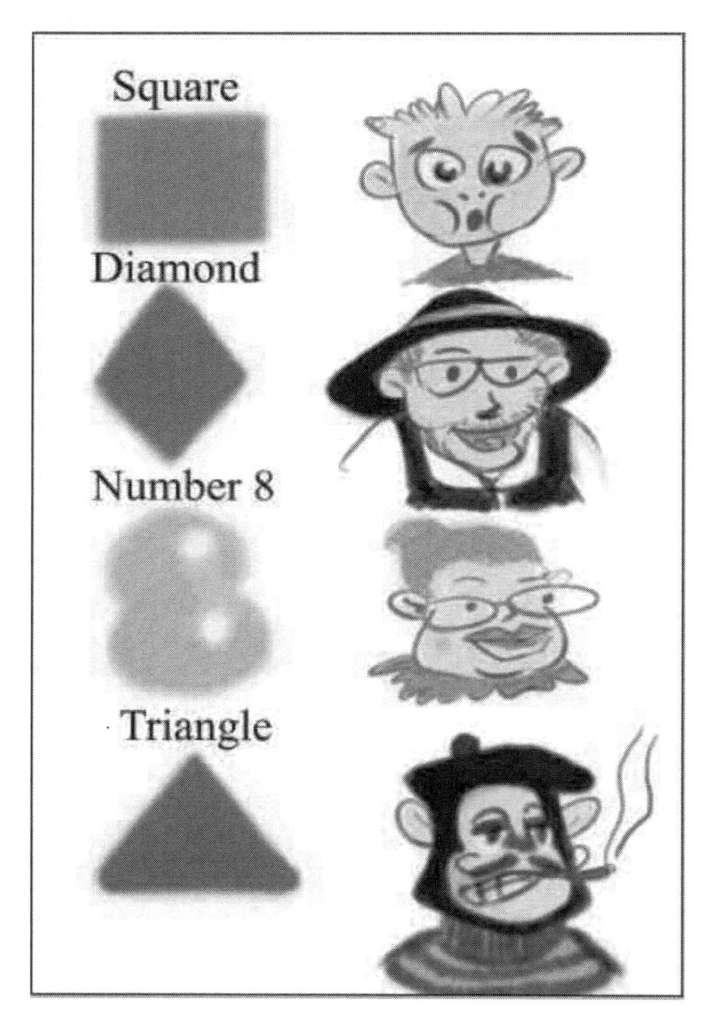

For your drawing practice, go outside your house and see people faces, and what is the shape of their face? is it a square...or rectangle?, distinguish it using your imagination, then draw them in your sketchbook, so draw another and another, that would be your reference when you need to draw a cartoon, so you see it is endless, so there is no reason for you not to draw what you see, and this is the skill that you have to cultivate if you want to draw cartoons.

Adding years to the Character

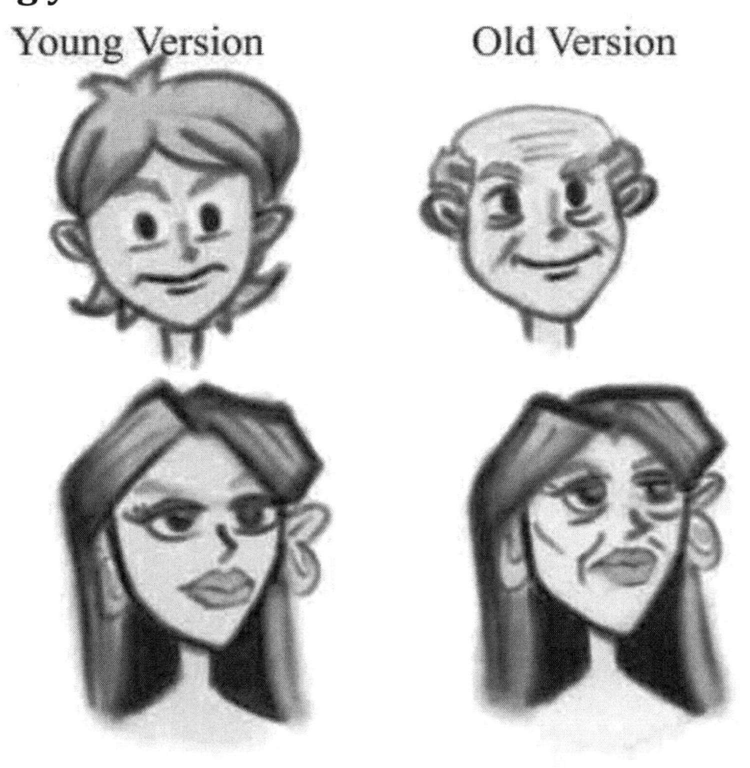

We can turn our character to an aged man or woman, by adding wrinkles to the face, so that means drawing some thin lines below the eyes and forehead as well the face. For a man you may also erase the hair so that the shiny head will be an evident of losing the hair an oldest trick used in the movies.

Cartooning a baby

1. Start with the wide circle, add a crosshair.

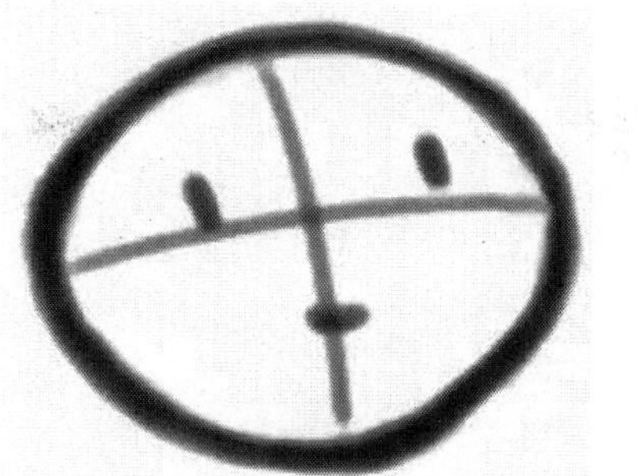

2. Draw the eyes, eyebrows, nose and mouth.

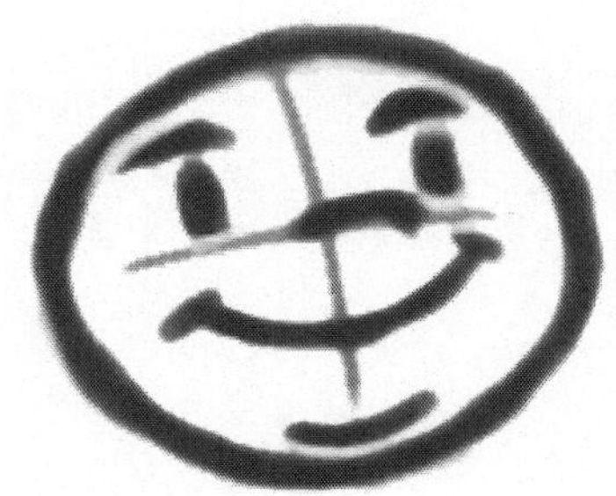

3. Add the hair and ears.

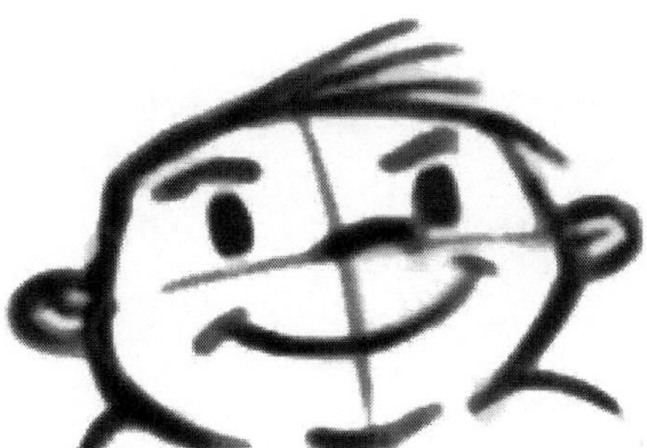

4. Erase the crosshair, and we have a baby's face.

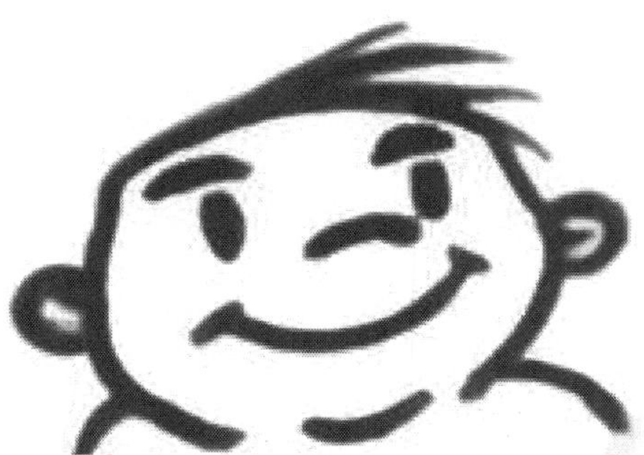

For the rest of the body, I will give a guide for the construction of the baby's body; we will discuss it later about how to construct the body in the next coming chapter.

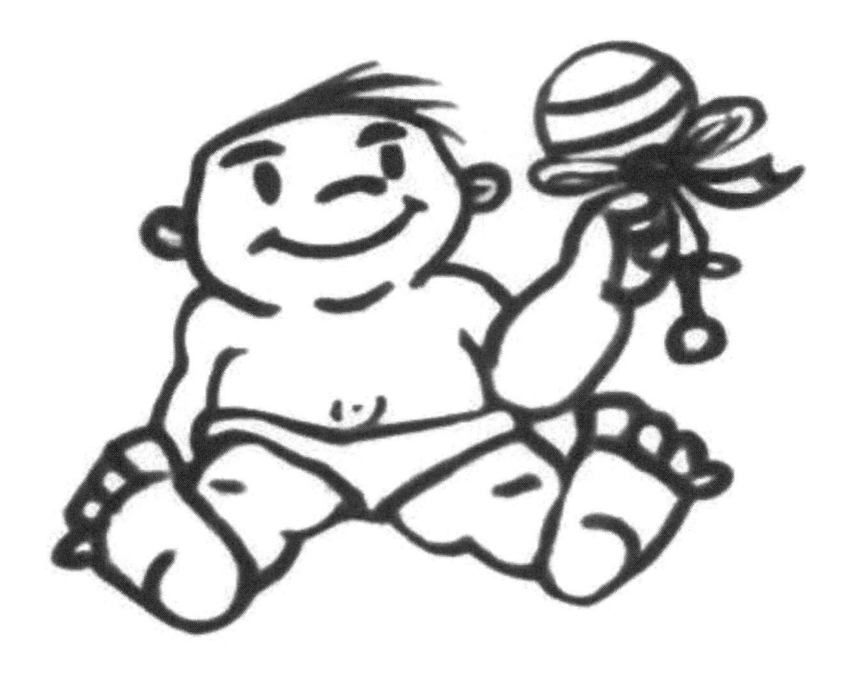

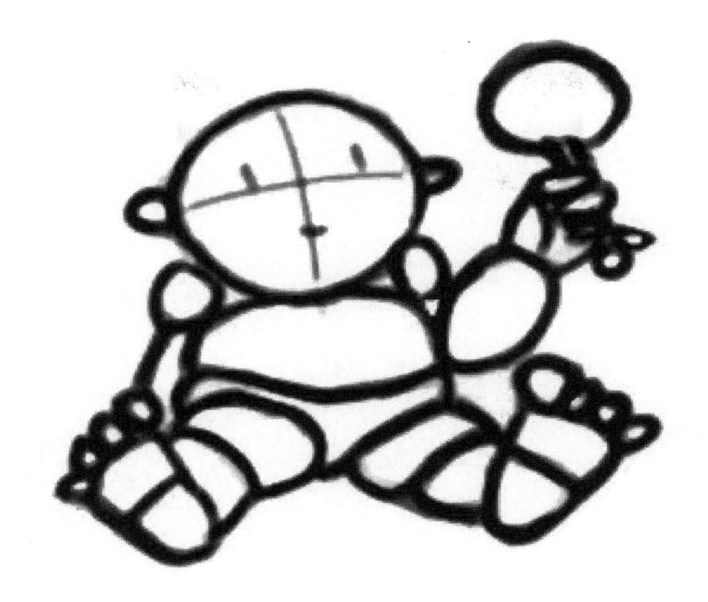

Drawing Cartoon Eyes

Here are the lists of cartoon eyes you can choose and use when drawing them, also I include the eyebrow.

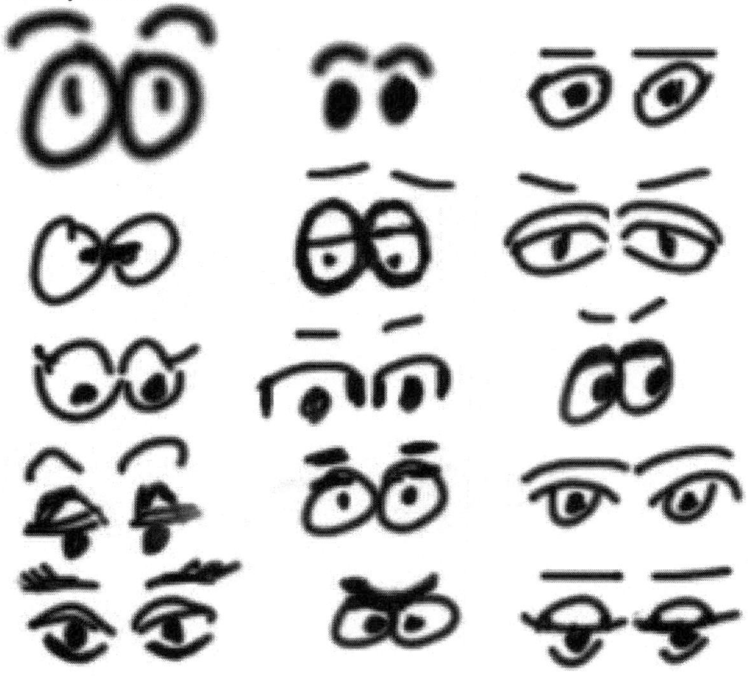

I'm sure there are many other cartoon eyes you can make, aside from what I provided; again you can go outside your house and try to observe the eyes of the people and imagine the basic shapes behind their eyes, and add it as our reference, so use your imagination.

Drawing Cartoon Nose

Here the list of the cartoon noses that can used when adding a nose to your character; with front and side view, keep it simple but make it crazy and loony.

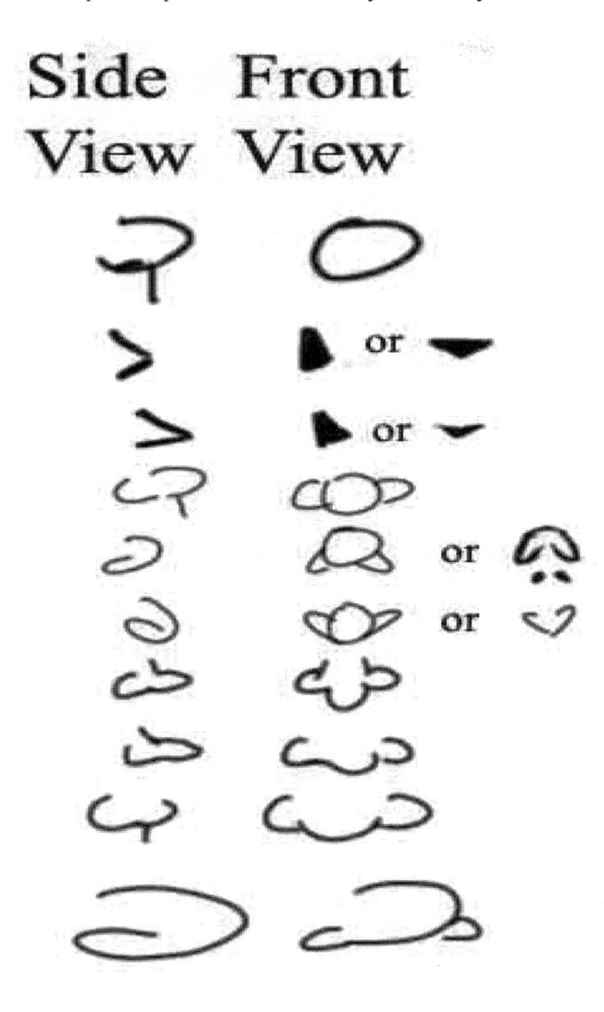

Do the same for the noses, like what we did on the eyes, observe shape of the nose of other people, and draw the shape in your sketchbook for your reference.

Drawing Cartoon Mouth or Lips

Mostly cartoon lips are just drawn by a simple thin line for a man (a.), for a woman full lips are used to indicate femininity (b.and c.).

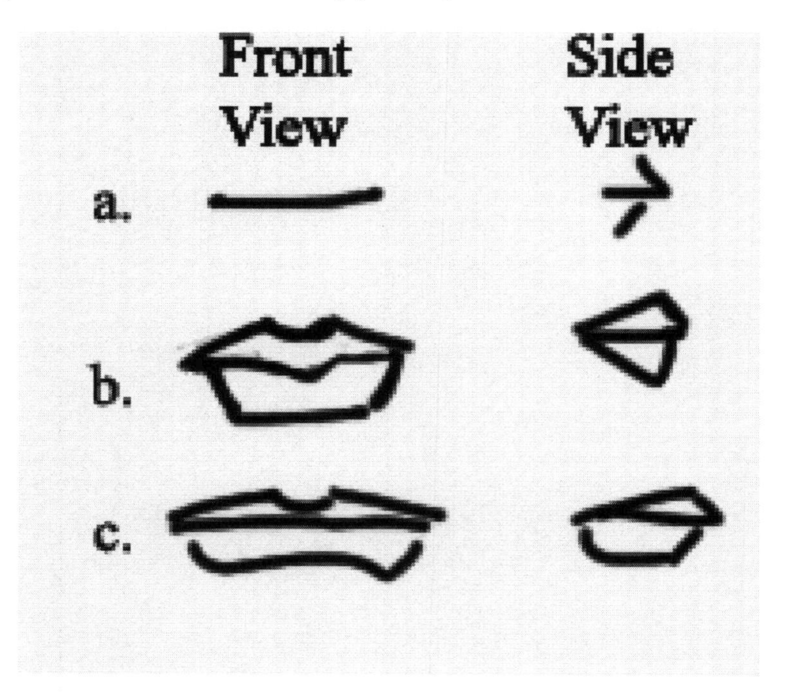

Drawing Cartoon Ear

The cartoon ear is easy to draw; its shape is like a letter C, with lots of Cs as you can see in our example below.

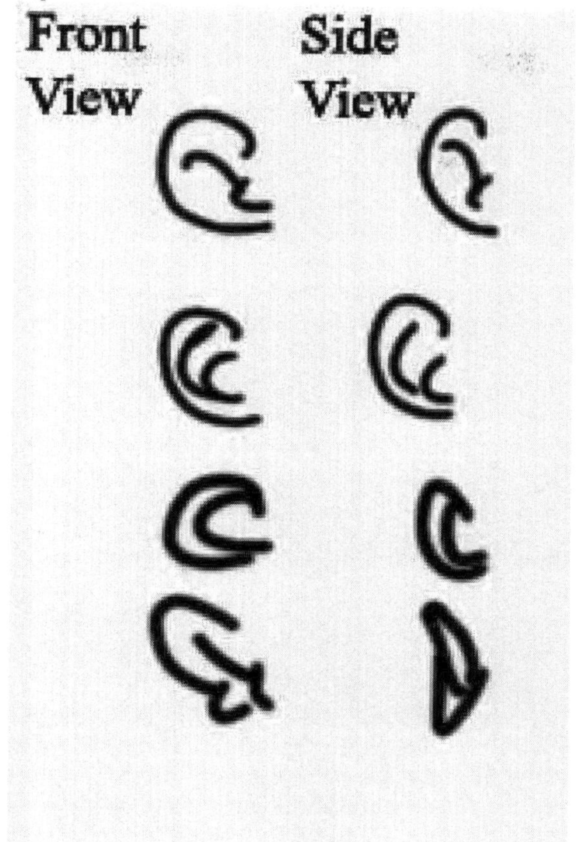

Expressions

Now we're finished learning the features of the face, let me teach you how to draw different expressions of the face to make it livelier.

a. Normal expression
b. Smiling or happy
c. Smiling with mouth slightly open
d. Laughing with full mouth open
e. Laughing in a normal degree
f. Sad
g. Crying
h. Upset
i. Angry
j. Extremely angry
k. Pondering

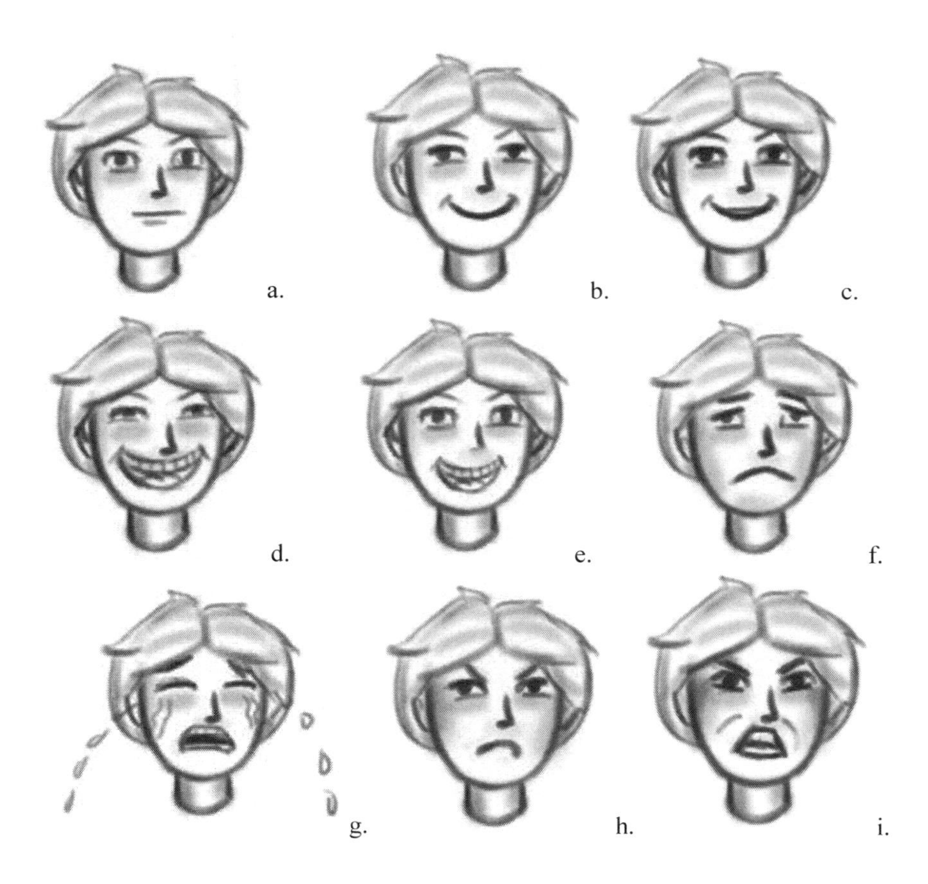

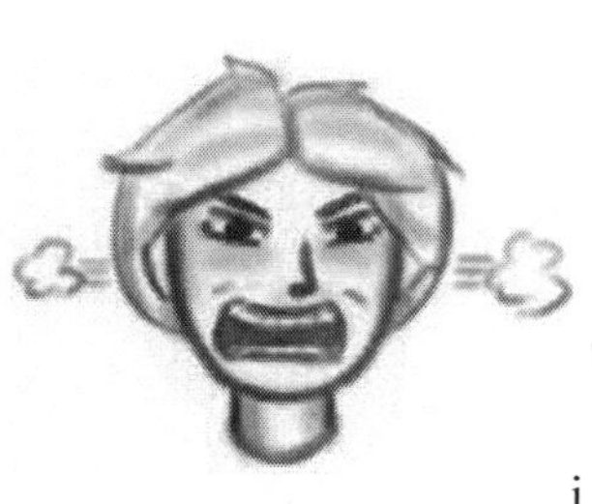

j.

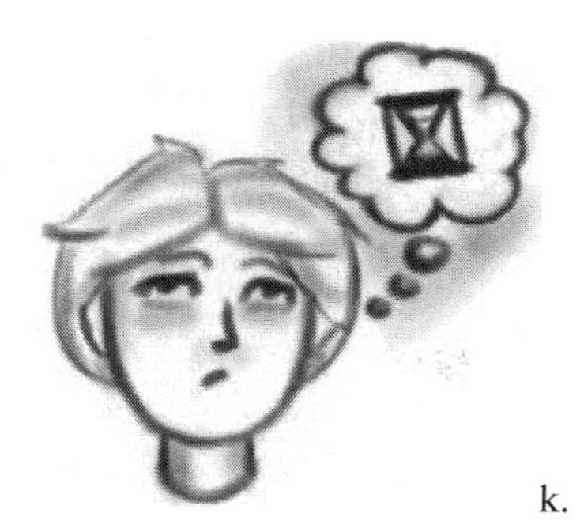

k.

Study these expressions, you may add more expressions and see how many expressions you can make, tip: you can draw more different expression by looking yourself in the mirror, and make some facial expressions, and draw it in the paper or your sketch book, these can also be your reference later on when you need it.

Drawing Cartoon Hands

Cartoon hands is different from real hands, usually they are drawn with four fingers including the thumb, there is no irregularity of the shape in the fingers as what you see in your hands it's evidently bony, in cartoons it's like you are drawing a tube or cylinder. Let me show you what I mean as we go along with the steps below.

Steps:

1. Draw a two big rectangular shape in a portrait orientation, and draw a rectangular shape beside it in a horizontal position. As you can see this is the framework for the hand one hand is the left and the other is the right.

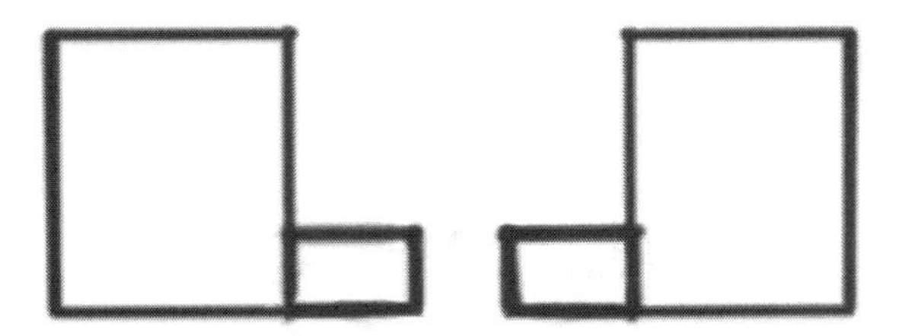

2. Divide the big rectangle on the top side by three parts, do the same to the other one.

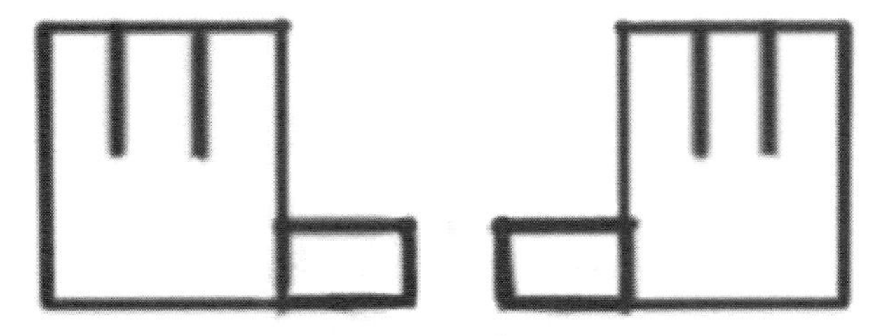

3. Erase the division line between the two rectangles. This is the back side of the hands, no need to draw the nails and the joints, remember keep it simple

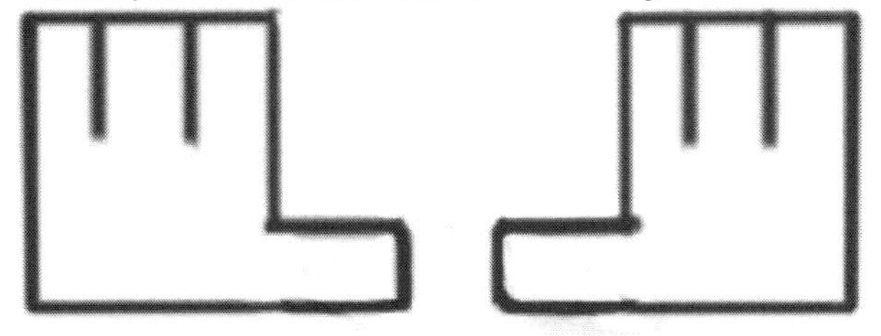

If you want to draw the other side or the palm of the hand it should be like this.

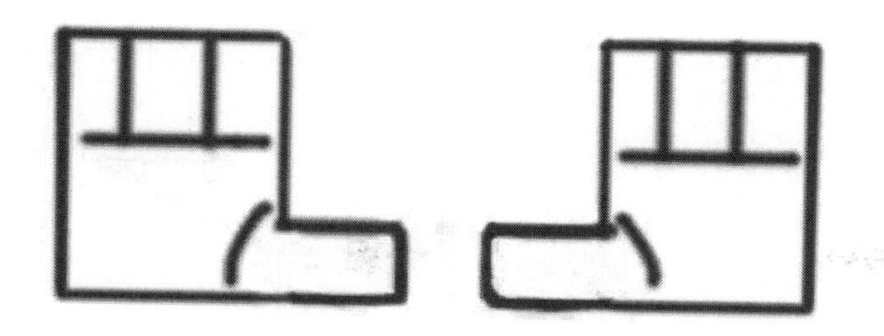

This is just the basic form and shape of hand, so that you will have a deeper understanding about the hands, now draw it but make it more loose and with curves (turn the stiff rectangle to a loose curves fingers and the side of the palm), and also draw the wrist remember to keep it simple.

Backside

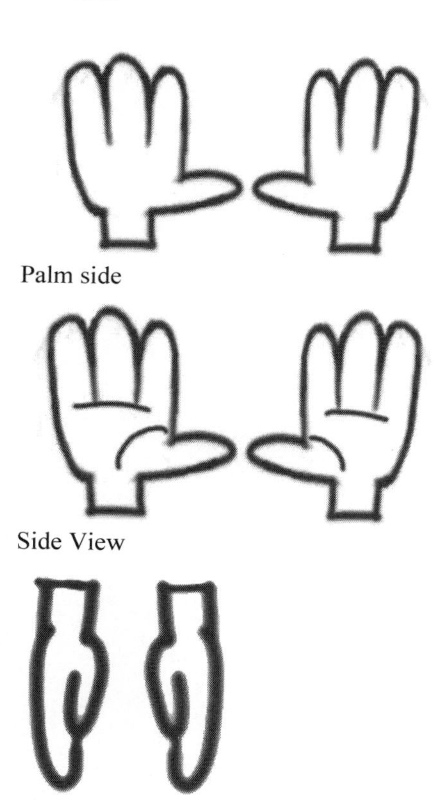

Below are long and slender hands including the fingers, draw this for women hands, it makes them more feminine.

Backside

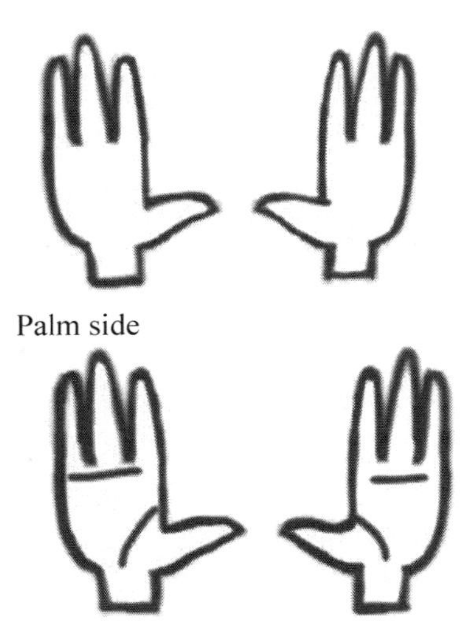

Palm side

Side View

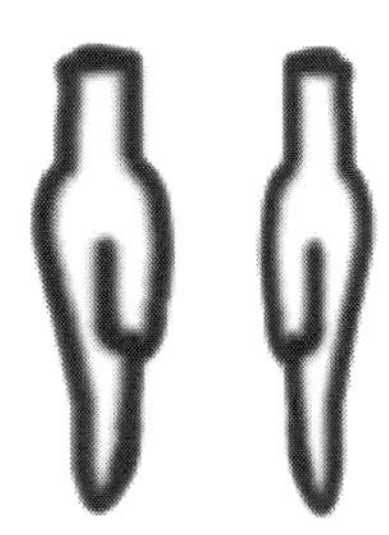

Knowing this basic knowledge of the hand, you can draw and add actions to any type of hand as you can see below.

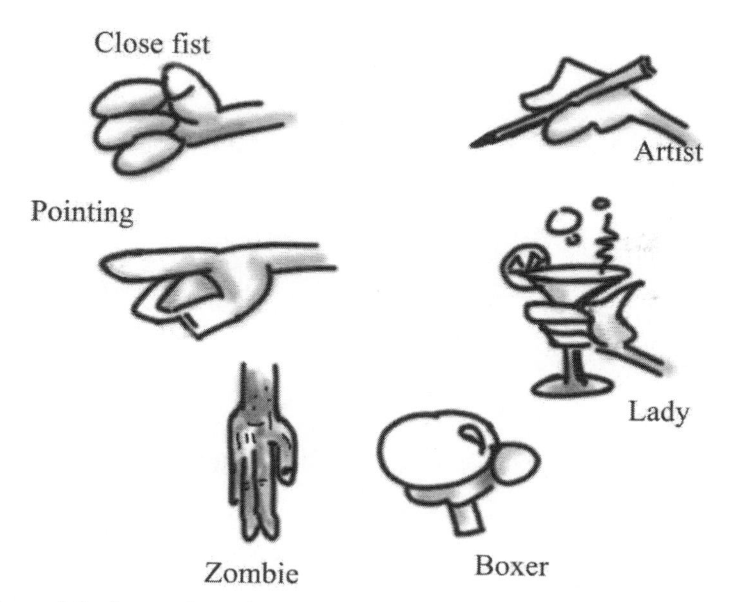

A good tip for you is to draw your own hand (not the dominant hand of course) or any hand that you see, pick any action of the hand and draw it, believe me it will help you a lot.

Drawing Cartoon Feet

Steps:

1. Draw two big boxes, on the top of the box place a small box do the same to the other box, see the placement of the boxes below.

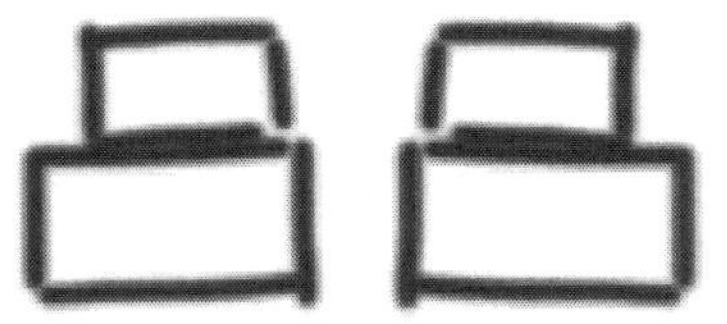

2. Then draw a small box inside the big box, this will be our big toe, dot the same to the other box.

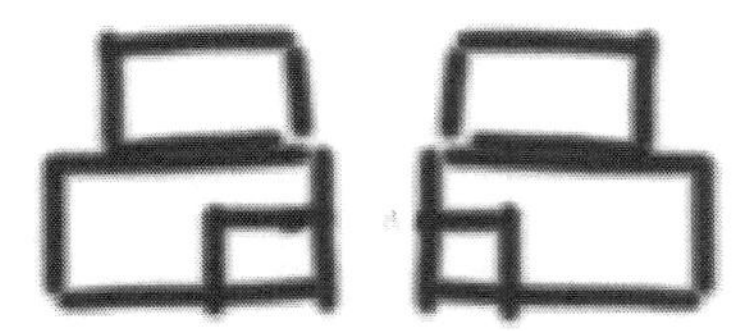

3. Draw two vertical line beside the box (big toe), do the same to the other box.

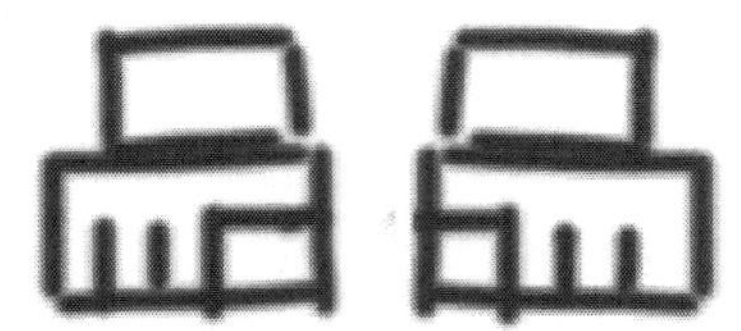

4. Erase the lines, and transform other lines to curves to make it loose.

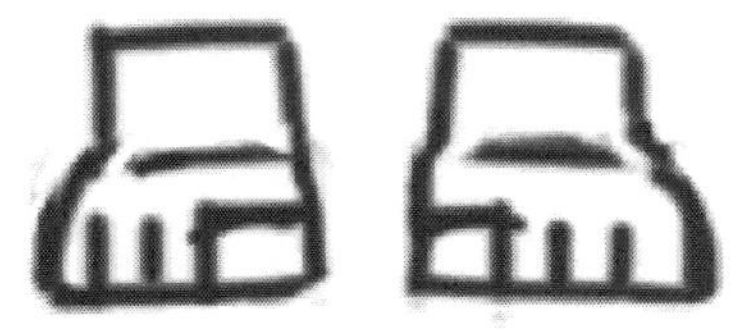

5. Continue to change the line to curves, and also change the other toes make them round like so that it will look like a toon. Also on the right side is the side view of the feet. Again let me remind you that since we are drawing a cartoon the feet have four toes. And a man's feet are bulky compare to woman.

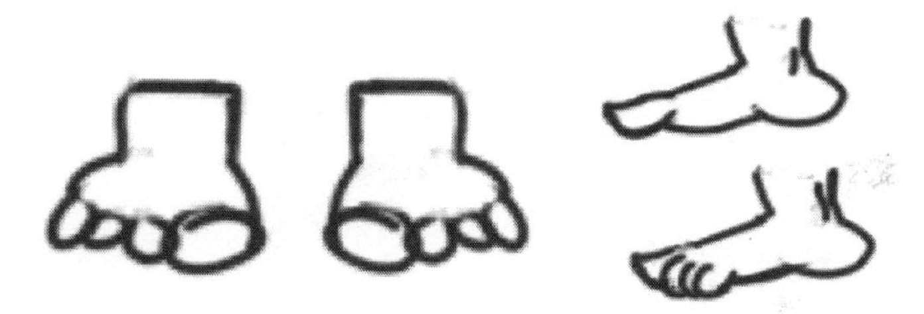

Man's feet bottom view

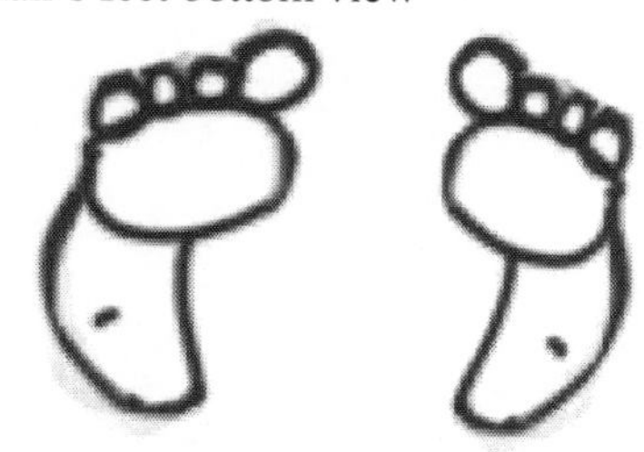

Below is a woman feet, see it more slim and seems light compared to man, again because of femininity and graciousness of the women.

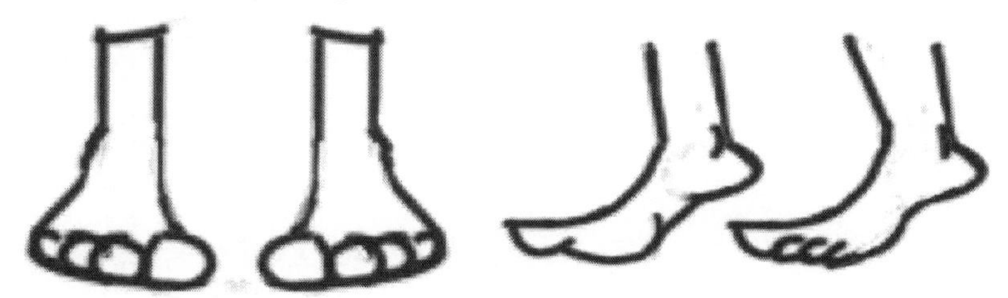

Woman's feet Bottom view

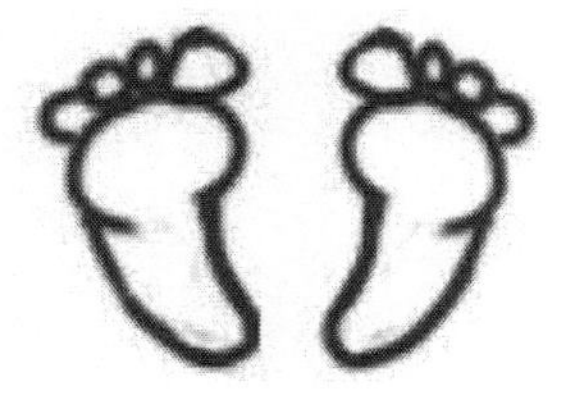

Below are various samples of what you can draw for the feet, you can draw a shoe to with different designs.

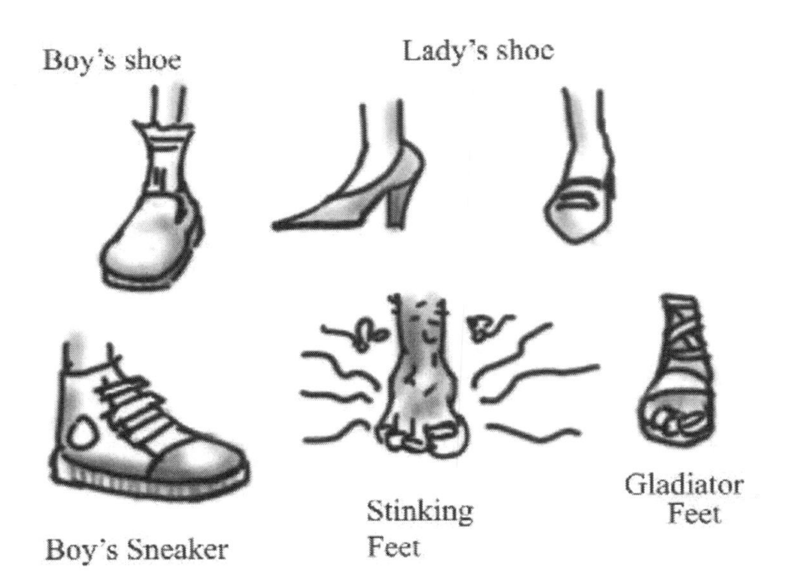
Boy's shoe
Lady's shoe
Boy's Sneaker
Stinking
Feet
Gladiator
Feet

Stick Figures

Remember the first time you were drawing a man or a woman in the paper, it's likely you're drew a stick figures.

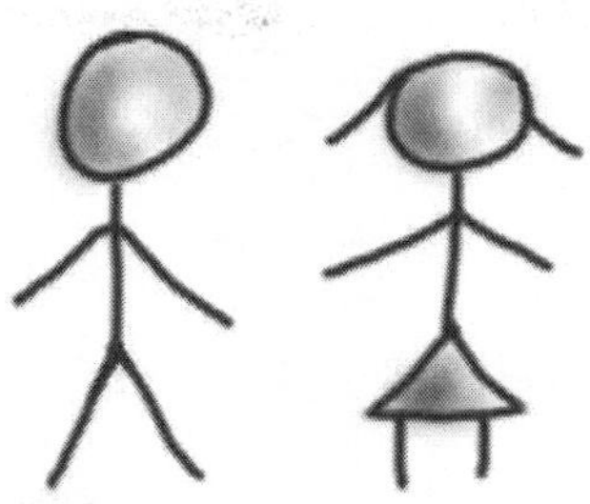

You may say it's so primitive, well let's make some modification, as what you see below we have the major composition of our new stick figure, it resemble a skeleton, but for our cartoon lesson let's stick to this simple figure and not to complicate it. We have an oval shape for the head, another one for the rib cage, and a laying oval for the pelvic, and the rest of the sticks are for the neck and extremities: arms and legs, don't forget to include the hands and the feet to make it figure complete. Draw, study the figure and practice drawing this figure to become familiarize with it.

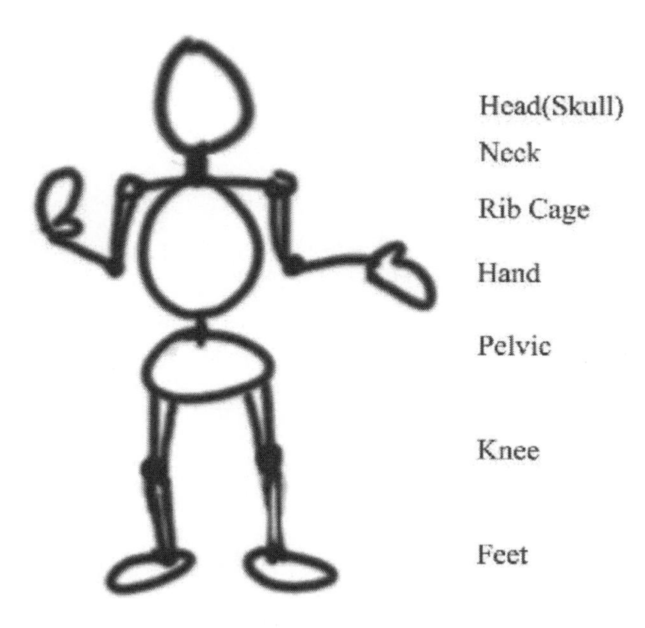

The Center Line and Poses

This act like a spinal cord for the cartoon characters or any animation, this is useful when drawing especially when making your cartoon character pose or adding some action to it making it more fluid.

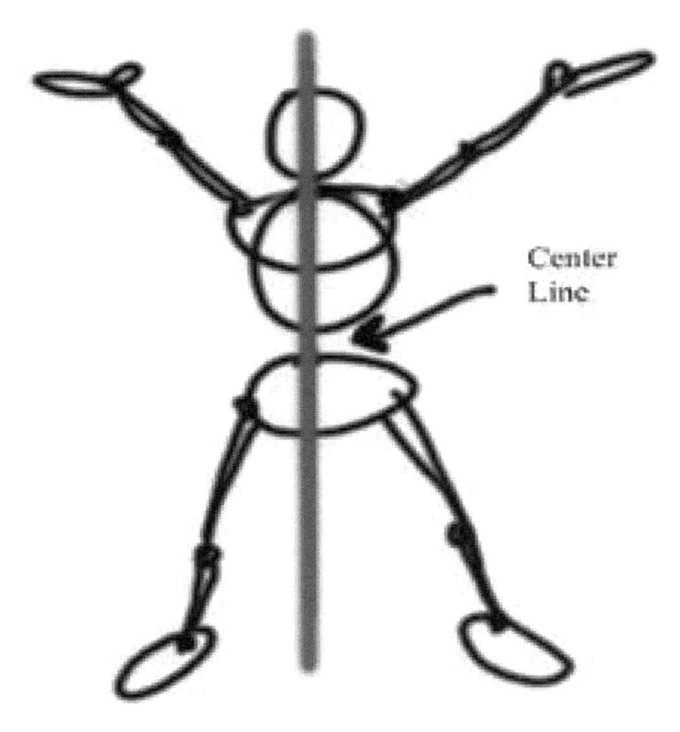

Below are various poses with the center line, see how is it important in drawing cartoons, yes it is the backbone of every character that you see in all the cartoons.

Light and Shadows

It's important to know about lights and shadow when drawing cartoon, even I mention before that in cartoons you can make things possible and we can bend rules, but with shadows you can add depth to your cartoons, provided you know the light source.

So let me introduce you to my friend, "Manny".. ok his just a wooden mannequin, but he is the only model available this day, so let's make the most of him, before he will change his mind and charge me with his Professional fee, he will even hunt me in my dreams, and I don't want that to happen so let's not waste time.

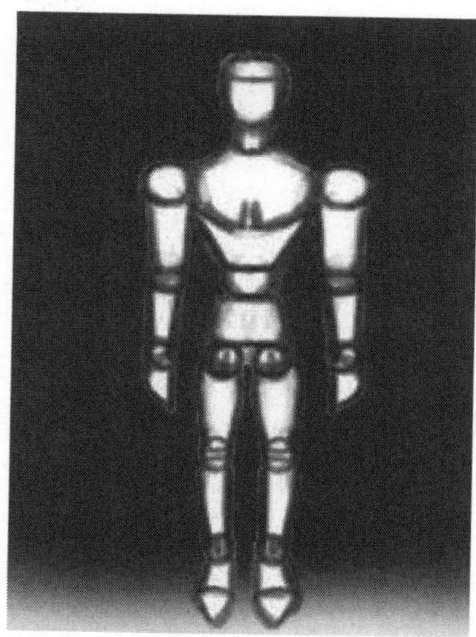

Let's as say the Light source is over Manny's head.

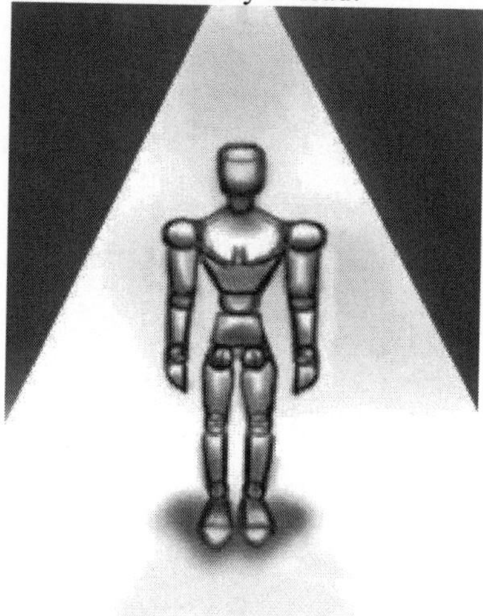

Most of the surface that are expose with light receives the light, notice the head and the shoulders have a spherical shapes, so the bottom portion doesn't receive light, so that is where the shadow will be(take note of the transition of light). The arms are cylindrical shape, notice how the light and shadows fall to it, shadows are on the sides of the cylinder because of its shape and that area is where the transition of light can be seen, and also in the lower portion where light can't reach that area. Also the abdomen area does not receive the light compared to the chest area which is directly over the light. Moving on to the other shape, the pelvic area has a square but with a curve area on the top where it receives light and below the curve does not. For the legs and calves it's the same like the arms since it is cylindrical shape, for the feet there are transition of light also, the ankle has shadow working its way to the toes where there is already light, and don't forget the cast shadow on the ground, since the light is directly on the head of Manny, the cast shadow would just be that size a little bit wider than both feet.

If the Light source is on the Upper left hand corner (a.), the shadow would fall on the right side and somewhat diffuse. So here you notice the change of the placement of the shadows, more shadows on the right side areas: on the head, shoulder, chest, arms, abdomen, legs and feet. Same thing if the light is on the Upper Right hand corner, shadow would fall on the left side, same with the other Shapes of the Manny's body(b.).

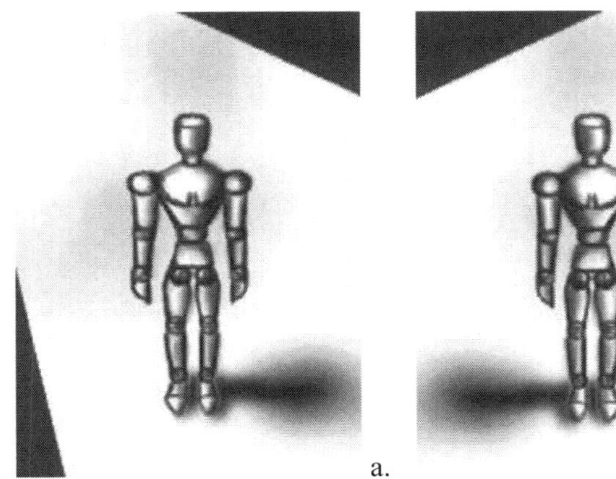

a. b.

Read our other books

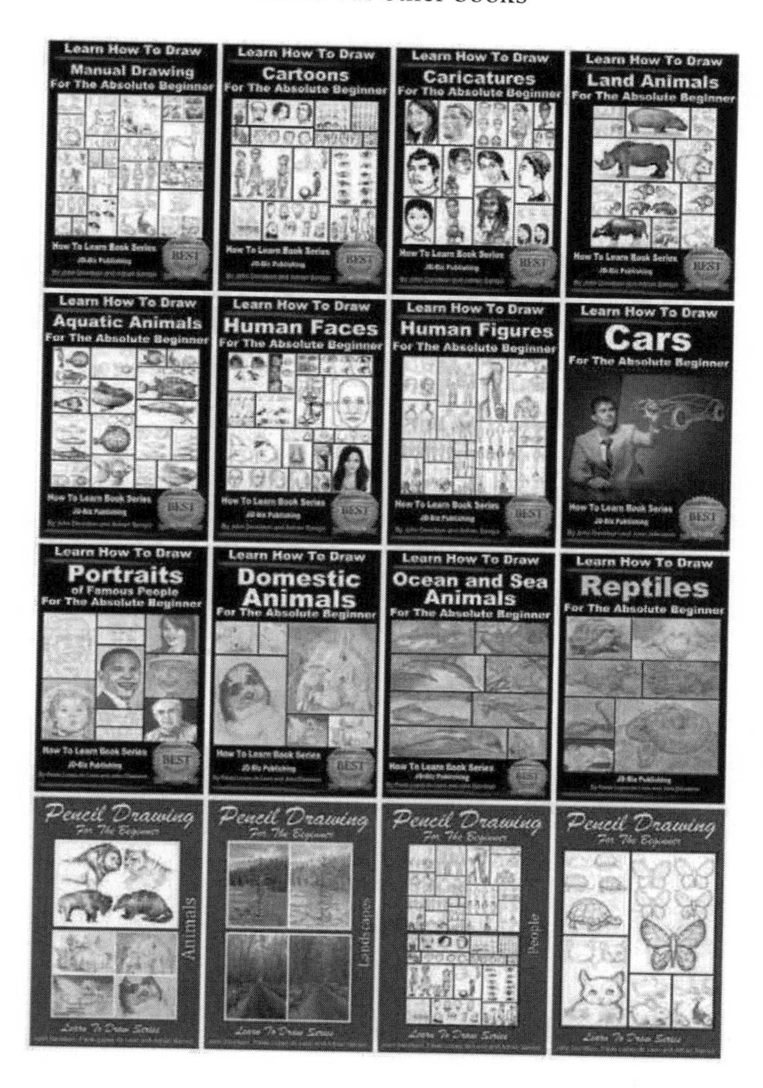

8517292R00035

Printed in Germany
by Amazon Distribution
GmbH, Leipzig